Heroes

Zach Hunter

Modern-Day Abolitionist

Q.L. Pearce

KIDHAVEN PRESS
A part of Gale, Cengage Learning

GALE
CENGAGE Learning

Detroit • New York • San Francisco • New Haven, Conn • Waterville, Maine • London

GALE
CENGAGE Learning™

Cover photo courtesy of Tom Sapp.

LIBRARY OF CONGRESS CATALOGING-IN-PUBLICATION DATA

Pearce, Q.L. (Querida Lee)
  Zach Hunter : modern-day abolitionist / by Q.L. Pearce.
    p. cm. — (Young heroes)
  Includes bibliographical references and index.
  ISBN 978-0-7377-4053-0 (hardcover)
  1. Hunter, Zach. 2. Teenage boys—United States—Biography. 3. Abolitionists—United States—Biography. 4. Social participation—United States. I. Title.
  HQ797.P43 2009
  326'.8092—dc22
  [B]
                                                                        2008026590

KidHaven Press
27500 Drake Rd.
Farmington Hills, MI 48331

ISBN-13: 978-0-7377-4053-0
ISBN-10: 0-7377-4053-1

Printed in the United States of America
1 2 3 4 5 6 7 12 11 10 09 08

Contents

A Shy Boy

Zach Hunter is a soft-spoken, likeable young man. Like many teens, he has several goals. He would like to play guitar, write music, and improve his serve in tennis. His main ambition is more surprising. He hopes to help bring about an end to modern-day slavery around the globe. Zach Hunter is an **abolitionist**.

Not long ago Zach stood on stage at the annual Creation West Christian Music Festival in front of a crowd of about 35,000 people. He told them about the **plight** of the world's slaves. He has voiced his message on countless television and radio programs, and his campaign to raise money to help free the slaves has spread around the world. By setting an example, Zach has challenged those around him to take a stand for freedom and to be a voice for the voiceless.

Zach Hunter, pictured in 2008, works to bring an end to modern-day slavery. *Photo courtesy of Daley Hake.*

Family Life

Zachary James Hunter was born in Bellevue, Washington, on November 8, 1991. "I have lived in Washington State, Colorado, and Northern Virginia as well as Atlanta. In Northern Virginia I lived pretty close to Washington, D.C., and got to see all of the monuments, museums, and historic locations. I also got to go inside the White House,"[1] Zach says.

He now lives in Lilburn, Georgia, a small suburb of Atlanta known for its charming historical district and the fall Lilburn Daze Arts and Crafts Festival. Zach's mother, Penny Hunter, is a marketing consultant. His father, Gregg Hunter, is an author and works in development for **nonprofit organizations.**

Zach also has a brother, Nate, who is seven years younger than he. "He's really tall for his age and is really outgoing. Like me, Nate has a strong sense of justice, and he has a tender heart for people who are

Zach Hunter is big brother to Nate, left, who is seven years younger than Zach. *Photo courtesy of Penny Hunter.*

6

being hurt," says Zach. The Hunter family also includes a lively Weimaraner dog named Riot who, according to Zach, "thinks she's human and loves to spend time with her people."[2]

Zach remembers that, as a young child, he liked playing with Lego building toys and enjoyed participating in many different team sports such as basketball, soccer, and flag football. He also realized very early in his life that people should always be treated fairly. "I remember how I felt when I'd see someone getting picked on at recess—especially if it was an older or bigger kid picking on a younger kid,"[3] Zach says.

Zach is now in his teens. His life is typical in many ways. He would rather play a video game than clean his room. He enjoys watching an occasional episode of the hit television show *American Idol*, and one of his favorite activities is listening to music. He likes many different styles, including the Christian rock music of Texas-based group Leeland and the progressive rock of San Diego band Switchfoot. Classic groups such as Kansas are also among his choices.

"I've just started taking guitar lessons and would love to be able to write and play music,"[4] Zach adds.

Another of his passions is reading. He hates to get rid of his old books, preferring to keep them and reread them over and over again. Although it is hard for Zach to single out a favorite book, there are a few titles that top his list. These include many nonfiction titles such as the diary of Frederick Douglass and anything by author Randy Alcorn, who has written several novels, including

Deadline, Dominion, and *Safely Home.* Zach particularly enjoys biographies, from the life stories of Rosa Parks, Martin Luther King Jr., and Benjamin Franklin, to the story of Iqbal Masih, a young **debt slave** from Pakistan who tried to take a stand against slavery.

Zach's taste in fiction ranges from satire to fantasy. One of his all-time favorite books is *The Screwtape Letters* by C.S. Lewis. He also really enjoyed the *Lord of the Rings* trilogy by J.R.R. Tolkien.

Much of Zach's free time is devoted to the many commitments he has made in his drive to end slavery. When he does have an opportunity to get together with friends, they go to concerts, take in a movie, or just hang out.

He also enjoys working on his tennis game as often as possible, and he is a member of his high school tennis team. Zach chose the sport because it is something that he can play throughout his life. He feels good about his progress but complains that he really needs to work on his serve.

High School Days

Zach currently attends Heritage Academy in Buford, Georgia. He enjoys school and likes to find ways to apply what he has learned. When he took Latin a few years ago, Zach realized that on a visit to Washington, D.C., he was able to read the inscriptions on monuments and the scientific names in the museum. Asked about his favorite subject in school, he considers before deciding that it is probably English.

Zach (right, front) is pictured with some friends who agreed to appear with him on the cover of his book *Generation Change*. *Photo courtesy of Penny Hunter.*

"I love to write and read books and poetry," he explains, "so English is a natural favorite for me. But, I'm also looking forward to taking European History next year."[5]

Zach is interested in and has studied some of the great leaders throughout Europe. He is particularly drawn to the stories of the abolitionists from the United Kingdom who had an impact on life in the United States. He has even been able to get some firsthand experience.

"I was able to travel to England and Scotland in 2007, and I'm looking forward to learning more,"[6] he says. A few years ago he would have been terrified at the thought of getting on an airplane to visit a foreign country or having to make conversation with someone he had just met. **Zach is still not thrilled with boarding a plane, but the chance to meet new people, learn about their lives, and speak up for the oppressed drives him to**

Zach, his brother, Nate, and his mother, Penny, along the bank of Loch Ness, a large lake in Scotland. *Photo courtesy of Penny Hunter.*

continue on. It helps that his mother or father travels with him and assists him on speaking engagements.

A Case of Nerves

"It's true that I had an **anxiety** disorder when I was in elementary school. I would get afraid and panic over little things and sometimes over nothing at all. It made it hard for me to go to school,"[7] Zach admits.

Sometimes Zach would feel sick to his stomach or he would have trouble breathing. He adds, "I was deathly afraid to get up in front of a class."[8] He says that with the help of his family, a counselor, and God, he was able to overcome this problem.

"Through my faith and some really good advice I began to release the anxiety."[9] Zach's devotion to ending slavery has required him to set aside his own fears. When he began speaking publicly he had to come to terms with his **stage fright.**

Learning About Slavery

At the age of twelve, Zach was a seventh-grade student at Christian Fellowship School in Virginia. He remembers that in February, during Black History Month, his class was studying the great abolitionists, including Harriet Tubman and Frederick Douglass. Part of the lesson was about the **Underground Railroad** and the people who risked their lives to help slaves from the southern United States reach freedom in the North.

Inspired by Others

Zach also learned about Martin Luther King Jr., a Baptist minister. King was one of the main leaders of the American civil rights movement and the youngest man to receive the **Nobel Peace Prize**. Zach was inspired when he learned how King had encouraged the use of nonviolent protest to address social injustice.

"He sacrificed himself to bring about a nonviolent revolution to defend the rights of all people,"[10] Zach said. William Wilberforce became another of Zach's heroes. As a member of the British parliament, Wilberforce had worked to **abolish** the slave trade in the United Kingdom. He finally succeeded in 1807.

The concept of slavery was a terrible thing to Zach. He was horrified by the idea that one person could own another. He admired the courage of the people who worked to end slavery. He thought to himself that if he had lived during the days of the Underground Railroad or the civil rights movement in the United States, he would have followed leaders like **Douglass** or **King**.

Modern-Day Slavery

One day during the drive home from school, Zach asked his mother, Penny, about her new job with the International Justice Mission (IJM). When she told him that the nonprofit organization helped to free slaves and raise awareness about **oppression**, Zach was amazed. He began asking her questions and learned that some of the people the IJM worked to rescue and defend were modern-day slaves.

Zach learned that slavery is a bigger problem now than it ever has been. Even though it is illegal everywhere, some 27 million people around the world are slaves. More than half of them are women and children.

A slave is someone who is the property of another person. Slaves are forced to work, but they do not get to keep the money they make or the things they produce.

Two child slave laborers in Nigeria work under grueling conditions breaking granite. *AP Images.*

They are often controlled through violence. Modern slavery includes the sale of children to settle debts, the unlawful use of child labor, and the use of children as soldiers. The most common victims are people who are poor. Sometimes loving parents cannot feed or care for their children. They might become desperate enough to sell their children into slavery. The slave trader might trick the parents by promising that their child will have a good job and thus be better off leaving the family.

Penny Hunter explained that slaves may be forced to work in fields picking produce or breaking rocks. They may labor in factories making bricks or rugs. The work can be dangerous and even deadly. Some children in Asia are forced to spend their days rolling little cigarettes called *beedis*. The harsh work can make their fingers raw.

When Zach's mother added that as many as 17,000 slaves are brought into the United States every year, Zach was stunned. "At first I was just really angry and sad," he admits. "But, then I realized that feeling bad just wasn't enough. I had to do something with my feelings."[11]

Zach's answer came from a passage in the Bible. "Speak up for those who cannot speak for themselves, for the rights of all who are destitute. Speak up and judge fairly; defend the rights of the poor and needy."[12]

"Slave owners are cowards," Zach says. "They take advantage of people . . . who don't have anybody to protect them."[13] He realized that the slaves could not speak for themselves. They are not free to make their own choices or to live their lives as they please. "They need someone . . . to speak up for them."[14]

Zach's Plan

Zach told his parents that he wanted to help end slavery. They understood his concern, but he felt that they were not sure how to encourage him because the task was so huge. Gregg Hunter, Zach's father, remembers saying, "Zach, you're 12. You're a bit young to try . . . and free slaves; you can't do that."[15]

But then Zach thought about what he had learned about the IJM. His mother had told him about its president, Gary Haugen. Haugen had been a lawyer when he decided that he wanted to do something to protect the rights of helpless victims of **abuse**. To help achieve that goal, he had started the IJM. Zach had an idea. Maybe he could do something to support the important work of that organization and others like it.

"I thought about it and prayed about it, and the idea just came to me to put together two underestimated

things: young people and loose change, and use them to bring freedom,"[16] Zach explains.

Zach learned from *Real Simple* magazine that there is $10.5 billion in loose change in American households. He began to think about how much good some of that forgotten money could do if it were put toward

Gary Haugen, right, founder and CEO of the International Justice Mission, speaks at a human rights conference in 2005 alongside Senators Sam Brownback and Hillary Clinton. *Mark Wilson/Getty Images.*

Inspired by the simple idea that loose change could add up to a lot of money, Zach decided to call his antislavery campaign Loose Change to Loosen Chains (or LC2LC). *Photo courtesy of Penny Hunter.*

the abolition of slavery. His plan began to take shape, and he knew it should be student led. He believed that young people might have fresh ideas and lots of enthusiasm.

When Zach told his family about his plan, they all pitched in and started searching for loose change in their own home. They were able to dig up about $200 worth. Zach was encouraged. It seemed that the idea could work. He believed that if his friends and fellow students knew how many people around the world were forced into slavery, they would be willing to help him to raise funds. He decided to call his campaign Loose Change to Loosen Chains.

Three

Be the Change

The next challenge was to get the support of the school administration. Zach needed their permission to launch his program on campus. He would also need student help to collect and count change.

Loose Change to Loosen Chains

When he began to tell others about 21st-century slavery, Zach's friends and classmates were as shocked as he had been. Many of them were sad and even angry. There were also a few who did not seem to care, but that did not discourage him. A large group of students were willing to get involved with the campaign. They were excited about doing something to make the world a better place. Zach points out that his parents had encouraged him to find a group of people who could help because it creates a sense of **community**.

As more young people joined the campaign, Zach saw that his idea was working. Toward the

The idea of collecting spare change from family and friends for a good cause excited the students at Zach's school. *Photo courtesy of International Justice Mission.*

end of February 2005, Loose Change to Loosen Chains was ready to go. Students asked for loose change from family, friends, and neighbors. By April 1, the students had collected more than $8,500 in coins, bills, and even checks. Zach was soon able to present the money in the form of a large check to a very grateful Gary Haugen.

Everyone was happily surprised when donations continued to come in throughout the month of June. Zach had been right. Once people heard about the plight of millions of helpless men, women, and children around the world, they wanted to help. It was clear that the campaign would continue.

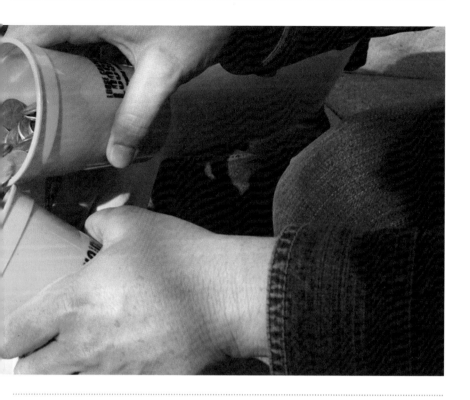

Zach Hunter presents Gary Haugen with a check from the first LC2LC fund-raising campaign. *Photo courtesy of International Justice Mission.*

He came up with a way to help students at other schools launch fund-raisers in their own communities. Business leaders soon lent support, and Zach found out about other organizations working to end slavery.

Spreading the Word

It was not long before Zach was asked to speak about the campaign to large groups. "The first time I went . . . on stage in front of a couple thousand people, I was really nervous,"[17] Zach said.

He realized then that he could walk out on the stage because of the slaves who needed him to speak out for them. He took a deep breath and remembered that it was not about him. It was about them. That gave him the courage he needed.

It became easier each time. After speaking to a group, Zach and his helpers passed yellow plastic cups for the audience to fill with change. When a friend gave Zach **shackles** bought from an international market, he used them as a visual aid. The shackles were made up of iron rings and joined by thin iron bars. Zach would hold up the re-

Zach holds a pair of iron shackles, which are often used to restrain slave laborers. *Photo courtesy of Tom Sapp.*

The once-nervous Zach now routinely speaks before large audiences. Here, Zach speaks to a group of young people at a music festival in Wisconsin. *Photo courtesy of Ted Haddock.*

straints in front of an audience. He showed how they prevented the person who wore them from moving freely.

Zach explained that the shackles are often used on children who work in factories in India where they are forced to roll the cigarettes called *beedis*. The children sit in one place for hours each day, inhaling cancer-causing tobacco dust. They roll three or four *beedis* per minute. If they are not fast enough, the master may beat the bottom of the child's feet until he or she cannot walk.

At a recent concert, Zach remembers being nervous about appearing before an audience of thousands. He

A student at John Brown University takes part in a Loose Change to Loosen Chains fund-raiser. *Photo courtesy of International Justice Mission.*

had been given time between music acts to talk with the spectators.

"Most of the people there were students, and they came and paid their money to hear music," he explains. "So, I wasn't sure if they'd pay attention. But, they were great."[18]

Yell "Freedom!"

At the end of Zach's message, he asked the audience to yell "Freedom" if they felt it was important for their generation to end slavery. The crowd screamed out "Freedom!" with a tremendous roar. Teen friend Christian David Turner worked with Zach at another event called Atlanta Fest. "I loved helping," Christian David says. "I felt excited . . . that the little thing I was doing would be important in the long run."[19]

Now more than 130 schools and churches have launched LC2LC campaigns of their own. Students in Africa, the United Kingdom, and Australia have also joined the battle to end slavery.

The money that students raise goes to one of the organizations Zach recommends. Each one of these organizations takes a different approach to ending slavery and aiding victims. Some of the funds support the work of undercover investigators who risk their lives to get **evidence** about the slave trade. Some money pays for the rescue of victims.

Funds may also be used for court costs, counseling, or the care of freed slaves. "Often they can't go back . . . because they've been disgraced by the work they were doing or because the family was involved in selling them,"[20] Zach says.

He tells audiences about a boy named Rakesh. The boy was one of many children who worked on a large **loom** weaving rugs from long wool strings. The slave owners used children because they have small fingers, and they can make the delicate designs that buyers like. Sometimes Rakesh would cut his fingers on the rough wool. Then he might be beaten for not working hard enough. Through the help of Free the Slaves, a group Zach supports, Rakesh was freed.

Money from LC2LC is never used to buy freedom for slaves. Zach points out that people are not property. It is illegal to buy a human being even if the intention is to set them free. Also, if slave traffickers continue to get money, no matter who it is from, they will continue to enslave people. Only law enforcement agencies can actually rescue victims. Several of the organizations that Zach supports provide care facilities and places where slaves can start their lives over.

Be the Change

Zach wrote a book called *Be the Change*, published in 2007. It is aimed at readers in their teens and twenties. In it, Zach explains that young people can make a dif-

Zach, pictured with his father, Gregg, credits his parents as his inspiration to follow his convictions. *Photo courtesy of Penny Hunter.*

ference in the world. He gives examples of people, some young, some older, who have made an effort to change the world for the better.

Zach describes the writing process as fast and furious, since he finished the manuscript in less than two months. "I had to come home from school every day and start writing."[21] Zach's second book, *Generation Change*, was published in 2008.

For inspiration, Zach turns to his mother and father. He also looks to the young men in the Christian rock group Leeland, whom he met at the Spirit West Coast Music Festival in Monterey, California. Performer and songwriter Leeland Mooring heard Zach leading a seminar and wanted to know more about the campaign. The band became **advocates** for slaves.

"My parents have set a good example for me of how to follow God," Zach explains. "And Leeland has showed me that God is as big as I had hoped he was."[22]

Four

A Voice for the Voiceless

Zach is no longer a stranger to publicity. He has been a guest on *Good Morning America*, CBN, CNN's *Faces of Faith*, and CNN International, and he was featured on the CNN Heroes campaign. He has also done several videos for student groups. Zach's message has appeared in *Newsweek*, *Weekly Reader*, *Breakaway*, the *Christian Science Monitor*, the *New York Times*, and many other print publications.

Speaking Out

"I've had the privilege of talking to many people in the media," he says. "And they have all been great about wanting to tell the truth about slavery and what each individual can do to help end it."[23]

Zach's main concern is that he tell the story of the people who are suffering in a way that maintains their dignity. Because his message is so important, Zach has not had a serious problem with stage fright for some time. His schedule does take a toll on him, though. Traveling and speaking can be tiring, and like any other teen, Zach has to get his homework done, too.

His mother and father are amazed at the change in Zach over the past few years. "Knowing that he puts himself aside . . . to speak out for others who don't have a voice, is truly remarkable,"[24] said his father, Gregg.

Zach may feel at ease on stage, but he is still a little shy when he is singled out for praise. Young people even ask for his autograph. Steve Carter, the youth pastor of Mars Hill Bible Church in Grand Rapids, Michigan, is impressed by Zach's quiet humility. He observed after Zach had spoken to the congregation of 10,000, "He's just himself, and I was really blown away by that."[25]

Although he is getting used to being recognized, Zach does not feel completely comfortable when he becomes the center of attention. He believes that the focus should always remain on raising public awareness of the plight of the slaves.

The Amazing Change

In 2007 Zach became the global student spokesperson for the Amazing Change, a social justice campaign. Slavery was abolished in the United Kingdom 200 years ago. The end was brought about through the efforts of

As student spokesperson for The Amazing Change, Zach encouraged people to sign The Petition to Abolish Modern Day Slavery. Here he rolls it out at a White House event on human trafficking. *Photo courtesy of Penny Hunter.*

William Wilberforce. To honor this success, filmmakers presented the story of Wilberforce in the movie *Amazing Grace*.

Zach's favorite scene in the film is a conversation between Wilberforce and a young politician named William Pitt. Pitt tells his friend that he wants to become the leader, or prime minister, of England. When Wilberforce says that he is too young, Pitt answers, "We're too young to know that certain things are impossible, so we will do them anyway."[26] In fact, at the age of 24, Pitt became the youngest prime minister ever to serve in England.

The Amazing Change campaign is designed to promote the modern abolitionist movement and to extend compassion and help in other ways that continue the work that Wilberforce started. By going to the campaign Web site, supporters can make a donation, learn about student-led efforts, and explore other ways to help.

The title of the campaign is named after a well-known hymn, "Amazing Grace." It was written around 1770 by John Newton. He was William Wilberforce's pastor, but he had once been a slave trader. "His story is pretty incredible," Zach says. "Students should check him out."[27] Zach explains that once Newton became a Christian, he struggled with the terrible things he had done. Finally, he wrote the song out of the feelings he was experiencing.

On Amazing Grace Sunday, February 18, 2007, people across the nation and around the globe joined together and sang the hymn. They prayed that the world's slaves might be free someday. Zach was pleased to be a part of the event. He was particularly happy to meet another guest, Randy Alcorn, one of his favorite authors.

"What If It Were You?"

When asked what keeps him going, Zach answers that if he were a slave he would hope that someone would work hard to free him. That is one of the things he thinks about when he begins to feel a little overwhelmed. People who are suffering in slavery cannot quit, so he refuses to quit. He admits that he plans to go to college in the future, though he is not yet certain what he wants to study. Still, he is positive that he will always be involved in abolition in some way.

Zach also hopes to continue to inspire young people. "I think it's important as a civil society to care about people regardless of how far away from us they live, what color their skin is, or how unfamiliar their problem might be," he says. "If we only care about people who are like us and who live close to us, are we really being kind and **compas-**

sionate?"[28] Zach is particularly concerned about children, especially those who have no one else to defend them.

Zach feels deeply that ending slavery can make the world a better place for everyone. He asks, "What would you want someone to do if it were you who were held in slavery? Or what if it were your mom, dad, or best friend?" He points out that slavery is wrong no matter who is in chains. "What if it were you?"[29]

Schools and churches across the United States—and also in Africa, the United Kingdom, and Australia—have become involved with LC2LC. *Photo courtesy of International Justice Mission.*

What Can Be Done?

By example, Zach has shown that young people can make a difference in a problem as serious as slavery. He points out that the Bible says even a child is known by his actions. "My dream is that my generation would be remembered for being the generation that abolished slavery throughout the world and that took care of the poor and oppressed."[30] Zach and the organizations he works with offer many suggestions for the young abo-

Following Zach Hunter's example, young people are making a difference every day in the fight to abolish slavery. *Photo courtesy of International Justice Mission.*

litionist. Zach says, "I believe our generation should launch a new peace, love, and justice movement—but this time, do it with God."[31]

Learn About Slavery

First, it is important to be informed. By reading and using the Internet, young abolitionists can educate themselves about the problem and tell friends and family what they have learned. Be sure that people understand that slavery is not a thing of the past.

A Special Day

Free the Slaves.net has established February 27 as Antislavery Day. Encourage friends and family to observe the day and think about the 27 million men, women, and children who live in slavery.

Raise Funds

Use the tools from LC2LC or the Amazing Change Web site to start a fund-raising campaign. Any money raised can be donated to the organizations that fight modern-day slavery or through The Amazing Change.

Create a Clapham Circle

William Wilberforce was part of a group of friends and neighbors called the Clapham Circle. They met often to discuss how to end slavery. In fact, they worked on nearly 70 causes such as helping the homeless and stopping animal cruelty. A young abolitionist can also hold meetings about modern-day slavery with friends or neighbors.

Spread the Word

Write a letter of protest about modern-day slavery to a school or local newspaper. Organize a letter-writing campaign to your representatives in Congress. Write a school report about modern slavery so that your classmates can learn about the problem. Organize a **vigil** to show support or remembrance. Invite friends and family to gather and light a candle for the world's slaves.

Choose Wisely

Certain products sold in stores may be made or harvested by slave labor. When products are labeled "Fair Trade Certified," they are guaranteed to be from workers who received fair wages. These include goods such as coffee, tea, sugar, and chocolate.

Finally, Zach suggests that young people can achieve a great deal by setting a good example for others. "Don't let anyone look down on you because you are young, but set a good example for those who are older than you."[32]

Zach adds that there are so many great things out there for kids to accomplish, but he encourages them to get involved with just one specific thing. He warns that taking on a lot of causes can be overwhelming. "Just

One way that consumers can do their part to fight unfair labor practices is to purchase foods labeled as "Fair Trade Certified," which are guaranteed to be from workers who received fair wages. *AP Images.*

pick one cause that you're really passionate about and do something for that cause,"[33] Zach says. He notes that throughout history, small, determined groups have been able to bring about huge, important changes.

Zach encourages young people to do whatever they can and simply reminds them that "anybody can make a difference and be a voice for the voiceless."[34]

Notes

Chapter One: A Shy Boy

1. Zach Hunter, interview with the author, June 18, 2007.

2. Hunter, interview.

3. Hunter, interview.

4. Hunter, interview.

5. Hunter, interview.

6. Hunter, interview.

7. Hunter, interview.

8. Quoted in Jana Riess, "Abolitionist Teen Speaks Out Against Modern-Day Slavery," *Publishers Weekly*, February 21, 2007. www.publishersweekly.com/article/CA6418085.html.

9. Hunter, interview.

Chapter Two: Learning About Slavery

10. Hunter, interview.

11. Hunter, interview.

12. Proverbs 31:8–9.

13. Quoted in Jeremy V. Jones, "End Slavery Now," *Breakaway*, June 30, 2007. www.breakawaymag.com/AllTheRest/A000000509.cfm.

14. Quoted in Wendy Griffith, "A Modern-Day Teen Abolitionist," CBN News.com, February

23, 2007. www.cbn.com/CBNnews/108 333.aspx.

15. Quoted in Griffith, "A Modern-Day Teen Abolitionist."

16. Hunter, interview.

Chapter Three: *Be the Change*

17. Quoted in Griffith, "A Modern-Day Teen Abolitionist."

18. Hunter, interview.

19. Quoted in Jones, "End Slavery Now."

20. Quoted in Jones, "End Slavery Now."

21. Quoted in Riess, "Abolitionist Teen Speaks Out Against Modern-Day Slavery."

22. Quoted in Courtney Lee, "Meet Zach Hunter—the Teenage Abolitionist," *Christian Today*, February 22, 2007. www.christiantoday.com/article/meet.zach. hunter. the.teenage.abolitionist/9640.htm.

Chapter Four: A Voice for the Voiceless

23. Hunter, interview.

24. Quoted in *Good Morning America*, "Just 15, He Leads Fight to Abolish Slavery," ABC News, March 15, 2007. http://abcnews.go.com/GMA/story?id=2 951434&page=1.

25. Quoted in Jones, "End Slavery Now."

26. Quoted in Jones, "End Slavery Now."

27. Hunter, interview.

28. Hunter, interview.

29. Hunter, interview.

30. Quoted in Jones, "End Slavery Now."
31. Zach Hunter, *Generation Change: Roll Up Your Sleeves and Change the World*. Zondervan: Grand Rapids, MI, 2008, p. 18.
32. Hunter, interview.
33. Hunter, interview.
34. Quoted in Jones, "End Slavery Now."

Glossary

abolish: To put an end to something.

abolitionist: Someone who supports ending a practice, particularly slavery.

abuse: The physical or mental mistreatment of a person or animal.

advocates: Those who offer support on behalf of others.

anxiety: Extreme nervousness.

community: A group of people with a shared area or shared interests.

compassionate: Showing sympathy for the suffering of others.

debt slave: A person sold into slavery to settle a debt.

evidence: Something that shows or proves that something is true or real.

loom: A device used for weaving thread or yarn into cloth.

Nobel Peace Prize: An award given to someone who has been outstanding in promoting peace.

nonprofit organizations: Organizations that do public service or charity work and are not set up to earn a profit.

oppression: Long-term cruel or unjust treatment.

plight: A desperate, difficult, or dangerous situation.

shackles: Iron rings and chains used to bind a prisoner's hands or feet.

stage fright: A fear of speaking or performing in front of an audience.

Underground Railroad: A secret organization that helped slaves in the United States escape to freedom.

vigil: A period of waiting, watching, or guarding.

For Further Exploration

Books

Zach Hunter, *Be the Change: Your Guide to Freeing Slaves and Changing the World*. Grand Rapids, MI: Zondervan, 2007. The book is divided into eleven chapters, each based on qualities such as passion or sacrifice. It includes quotes, facts about slavery, discussion questions, and plenty of ideas about how to bring about change for the better.

————, *Generation Change: Roll Up Your Sleeves and Change the World*. Grand Rapids, MI: Zondervan, 2008. Zach Hunter's second book includes stories about students successfully working to change the world around them for the better.

Q.L. Pearce, *Given Kachepa: Advocate for Human Trafficking Victims*. Detroit: KidHaven, 2007. A victim of human trafficking himself, Given became an advocate for other victims.

Web Sites

The Amazing Change (www.theamazingchange. com/overview2.html). Lists ten things you can do that will make a difference. Has discussion guides, banners, and a fund-raiser tool kit.

Free the Children (www.freethechildren.com/index.php). A network of children helping children.

Free the Slaves (www.freetheslaves.net/NETCOMMU NITY/Page.aspx?pid=302&srcid=299). Activities and worksheets for upper elementary and middle grade students.

International Justice Mission (www.ijm.org). Learn stories of modern-day slavery and how you can help.

Loose Change to Loosen Chains (www.lc2lc.org). Download everything you need to start the Loose Change to Loosen Chains campaign in your community, including posters, PowerPoint presentations, press releases, and T-shirt order forms.

National Underground Railroad Freedom Center (www. freedomcenter.org). Students can see how history impacts the present and the future and can learn more about modern-day slavery.

Rugmark.org (www.rugmark.org/home.php). A site dedicated to ending child labor in the rug and carpet industry.

Index

About the Author

Q.L. Pearce has written more than 100 trade books for children and more than 30 classroom workbooks and teacher manuals on the topics of reading, science, math, and values. Pearce has written science-related articles for magazines; regularly gives presentations at schools, bookstores, and libraries; and is a frequent contributor to the educational program of the Los Angeles County Fair. She is the assistant regional adviser for the Society of Children's Book Writers and Illustrators in Orange, San Bernardino, and Riverside counties and is a member of the advisory board for California State University–Fullerton's Writing for Children program.